Web Design: Using iWeb®

A Step-By-Step Guide to Creating Your Website

George L. Strout

DEDICATION

This book is dedicated to Pat for all the help and support a person could wish
for.
Thank you

CONTENTS

ACKNOWLEDGMENTS

The continuing support and encouragement of my family and friends have made this project possible. They know who they are and how very important they have been to me.

Introduction

Welcome to the world of web design! In a very short time, you will be building your own professional-looking website. Having your own website can expand your personal and professional presence on the web. You can link your website, blog and Facebook page into an interlocked grouping that gives you and your contacts a professional and impressive web identity. Using iWeb® makes it fast and easy to do on your own.

Why create your own web site?

There are many reasons for creating your own web site. If you are engaged in any business from your own lawn service to house painting or running a small store, having your own site that you manage and control will help establish your presence in the community.

If you are involved in a volunteer organization or church, you can supply a web site for your club or organization very reasonably and have fun maintaining it for the group.

In today's world, families and friends are often living in different parts of the world. A family web site can be a great way to keep in touch with each other and share photos and events. Consider having a blog page for each family member where they can post entries and photos relating to their activities and thoughts. Each blog can be a different theme, which reflects the individual personality of the writer. The combined web site will help to inform other family members across the country or around the world of what is happening "back home."

This could be especially helpful to military families.

To see what kind of site you can build, visit:
http://web.me.com/GLStrout/GLStrout/Welcome.html

This book will get you familiar with the ease and convenience of using Apple, Inc.'s iWeb® program to publish your website. The program is well designed and easy to use. It has a nice help area but you have to know what questions to ask to find the information. The purpose of this book, is to give you a step-by-step guide to the main features of iWeb® and help you get a website up and running as quickly as possible. You will learn some new terms and techniques as you work through the steps but none of it is difficult or mysterious. In a few hours, you will have your first website "published" to a local folder so you can test it and see how it will perform on the Internet.

I have used several different themes in the demonstrations presented here. All the themes provided by Apple® work the same and you can feel free to choose the theme that best reflects your taste and personality. You will be able to follow the steps with any of them. As you progress, try different options and be sure to save the changes you like. If you try a change and it displeases you, you can either go back by choosing "undo" in the Edit menu or simply quit iWeb® without saving and re-launch it with the last version you had saved. Remember you cannot break anything here. In the worst case, you may have to do it again.

As you gain confidence and experiment, you will be bolder about your choices. The video I suggest you watch at the beginning of Chapter 1 gives you an overview of the iWeb® process and capabilities. This book attempts to pick up from there and lead you through the process to achieve the results the video shows you. By the end of the book, you will have learned how to create your unique presence on the Internet and, unlike a Facebook page for example, your website will be totally your own creation and stand out from the crowd.

You are about to discover the fun and creative expression possible with this powerful Apple® application. Relax and enjoy the adventure, you are about to create your own identity on the web.

1 THE BASICS

iWeb® is Apple, Inc.'s easy to use webpage creation program that allows the user to design and build a unique website for personal or small business use. The built-in templates are only the beginning of the possibilities. Once you have learned to navigate through the supplied options, there is a whole world of possibilities beyond that point that will allow you to create a professional looking and smoothly operating website. Take a few minutes to become familiar with the basics and you will be hooked on your newfound capabilities as a web designer. It is fun, easy and creative.

Starting on the new journey: Basic Features

Go to the Applications folder and open iWeb® by double-clicking on the

iWeb® icon .

If you have not signed up for MobileMe, you will get a window asking if you want to set it up. For now, say "No thanks", check the box that says, "do not show again" and go on to iWeb®.

If you do not see the screen below, you can find the video under Help on the menu bar. Go down to "Getting Started" and click to see the video.

Take a few moments to watch the video and get familiar with the basics. For reference, keep this website in mind. It contains several other videos that will come in handy as you develop your site.

User Tip: If you have opened iWeb® before, the Welcome Screen may not appear. Go to Help and scroll down and choose "Getting Started" to see the video link.

Now that you have watched the video, you may be eager to get started on building your new site. Apple® has provided you with some very professional templates to get you started but you will probably want your site to be unique and reflect your personality and taste. That is where this book comes in. It will take you beyond the basics and teach you how to customize your site in some more creative ways beyond what Apple® has shown you.

User Tip: If you get lost or confused, you can usually find your way again by going to the top menu bar and looking under view. If you are totally lost, go to Help> iWeb® help to find the topic you need to get back on track.

Choosing your theme

You may be greeted with the Theme Menu (Figure 3). If not, on the menu bar at the top of the screen, click on "File" and choose "New Page:" or "New Site."

User Tip: There are usually at least two ways to arrive at the same point in iWeb®. You can either use the menu bar at the top or the icon menu along the bottom of the screen. In addition, there are keyboard shortcuts shown along the right side of the drop down menus. For example: command c is the shortcut for copy and command v is the shortcut for paste.

The iWeb® program will present you with a menu of themes. As you can see, there are several themes to choose from and each theme contains eight different templates. You will use all or most of these templates as you build your website.

Theme Menu

User Tip: When you choose a theme for your website, you are not restricted to just that one theme. You can mix and match the "Welcome" page from one theme with the "About me" or Blog page from another theme, for example.

Take a moment to browse the available themes. Then choose the theme you would like to start with. Now the fun begins. In the left side bar menu, you should see a red and white cloud icon with the word "Site" beside it. For this tutorial, we will use the "White" theme as a basic canvas to work on. Choose the "Welcome" page. Click on the welcome page and a yellow outline will indicate the page you have chosen. Click on the "choose" button. The page will open in its own window and you will see a photo and some nonsense text. These are just placeholders and you will now start to personalize this page. At the very top of the page is the word "Welcome." This is the menu bar where each page title will appear as you build your website.

Just for fun, click on the highlighted welcome label at left and change the name of the page to "Home" then hit the return key. When you do, you will notice that it also changes in the menu bar at the top. You will discover that every element about the page is changeable. This is true of all pages you build.

Adding a photo

The text and photos on this page are easily changed. At the bottom, right corner is a "Show Media" button. Clicking on that will reveal the media panel. Across the top, you will see Audio, Photos, Movies and Widgets. You are currently interested in Photos.

When you choose "Photos", you will have two choices: either iPhoto® or photo booth, if you have it on your system. Photo booth will make active the built-in camera on your iMAC and allow you to take a photo or video to add to your website. For now, choose iPhoto® and choose one of the images you have stored in your photo files. Simply click on the photo you want and drag it to the photo on your web page template. It will automatically size to fit the placeholder photo you are replacing. If you want to change the photo, simply drag and drop a different photo over the one you just placed there and it will become the new image.

User Tip: If you try to choose a photo and there are none available from iPhoto®, save and quit iWeb® and launch iPhoto® then re-launch iWeb® and choose Photos again. Now you should see all the photos you have stored in iPhoto®. You can also drag and drop photos from your desktop or any other file to the iWeb® page.

Changing Text

Adding your own text to the webpage is just as easy. Simply highlight the placeholder text on the page and type in your new text. It will be formatted the same as what you are replacing. If you click once at the end of the header that appears below the photo, you will notice the outline of a box. This is the "text box." Click twice rapidly and the text will be highlighted. Now, just type your own text here. The same is true for the paragraph of gobbledygook below the header. Type in a welcoming message for your new website.

Adding photo and text

Now that you have added a photo and some text, there is a great way to try out other themes on the page you have just created. Before you start, go to File and Save. Then, be sure that your "Home" page is highlighted in the left side menu and click on the "themes" icon at the bottom of the window. A panel will appear with all 28 themes displayed for the "welcome" page. Choose one you would like to see applied to your welcome (Home) page and click on it. Your welcome page will change to the new theme. It may require some changes to exactly fit but it will give you a quick idea of how that theme would look with your content.

Once you try the theme go to the edit menu and scroll down to "Undo Change Theme" and your original page will reappear. Browse through as many themes as you wish to try them out and then proceed with building your website. As you build each page you may want to try this out to pick the most appropriate look for your content. Remember, you do not have to use the same theme all the way through your site. Some people like to keep it the same to establish a specific look to their site but that is up to you.

When you are happy with the way the page looks, be sure to save before you start building another page for your website. The new pages are just as easy and add interest to your site. After we add a few more pages, we will come back and do more customizing while we explore the power of iWeb®.

Adding pages to the website

Now that you have your Home or welcome page, choose the next page you would like to add. Clicking on the "Add page" icon at the bottom left will bring up the theme menu and show the other pages in the same theme as your first page. For now, choose the "About Me" page from the same theme. Click once on the image and then click on the "choose" button. In the left side menu bar, a new page appears with the name "About Me." The page title also appears at the top of the page in the menu bar for the website. It now reads "Home   About Me" with "About Me" in bold letters. That tells you that you are on the "About Me" page.

Suddenly, there is much new information to deal with here. It is completely editable and you can add or eliminate any element you choose. Start by putting in the information you want to include about yourself.

Highlight the name that appears here and type in your name. If you do not want to include your age, for example, simply highlight and delete that category and number that goes with it. If you hit delete twice, it will rearrange the categories and eliminate the blank line.

Change the photo to whatever you choose; this is a good place for your favorite photo of yourself. Add whatever heading and text you like below the photo. A brief biographical paragraph might be a good idea here. Remember, you are posting to the web so everyone, both good and bad, Friends and people unknown to you, can read what you write about yourself. Do not write anything you would not want the whole world to read on the front page of the local newspaper. Skip the photo albums section for now. We will add more pages and then come back to that. Go down to "My favorite links."

Adding links to your website

It is easy to add links to your site.

First, launch your web browser and go to your favorite site. For this exercise, I chose Apple.com.

Next, go back to your iWeb® program and click on "inspector" at the bottom of the window. This will give you a lot of information about your web page. For now, go to the blue circle with the white arrow in it and click on it. It will be the seventh tab at the top of the inspector panel. Just below the "T" tab, you will see two other tabs: Hyperlink and Format. We need Hyperlink.

Now, go over to the "about me" page and highlight the text under the heading "My Favorite Links." Type in the name for the website you have chosen. In this case, I typed "Apple Inc." Take your cursor and highlight the text you just typed.

Here comes the magic. Click the box to "Enable as a hyperlink." In the drop-down menu choose " an External Page" if it is not automatically chosen. The URL of the page you opened in your browser should automatically appear in the next line. If it does not, copy it from the browser and paste it here.

Check the box that says "Open link in new window."

Check the box that says "Make Hyperlinks active", go over to the webpage your building, and click on the new link. It should open a new page in your browser and take you there.

Congratulations; you are now linking to the web! Add any other links you wish and your about me page is done for now. We will fix the album links after we build the album pages. For now, your page should look like this:

About Me page

User Tip: You can add a link to any page or website you want simply by highlighting the work or image that you choose to represent the link and following the steps in the Hyperlink Inspector.

Now, add another page. Go to the "add page icon and choose the "My Albums" page. Remember, you can choose to add a page from a different theme if you wish or keep all your pages from the same theme.

Adding Photo Albums

Again adding a photo album is easy. Once you have the "Album" page added, simply go to the Media menu and choose photos at the top. In the window just below the top menu, is a window that displays all the albums you have created in iPhoto®. Just drag and drop the album you want on the placeholder album on your new webpage. As the program adds the album, it will automatically open the album displaying the photos in that album. This is a good time to go through the photos, arrange and label the ones you want to display in iWeb®. As you highlight a photo you do not want, hit the delete key and it will disappear from your webpage but it will not be deleted in iPhoto®.

If you want to add more albums, click "back to index" if the album is open and just drag them to the space next to the first album. This will create another separate album beside it. For now, limit yourself to one or two albums. You can add more later when your website is finished.

Now, it is time to link the new albums to the About Me page. Again, you can simply add any text you wish, such as "See my Travel Album" and, use the Hyperlink Inspector to make a link to your album page.

In the left side menu, click on the About Me page.

Go to the section labeled "My Photo Albums" and highlight the placeholder text on the first one. Type in the name of your first album and then highlight it.

Open the inspector window and choose the link tool that you used to make your other links earlier and follow these steps:

Click the box to "Enable as a hyperlink."

In the drop-down menu choose "one of my pages."

In the next drop-down menu scroll down to the name of the album you want.

Check the box that says "Make hyperlinks active"; go over to the webpage you are building, and click on the new link. It should open your album.

Now, repeat the process for each album you have added to your webpage. You can drag and drop any photo from your iPhoto® (in the media menu) to the photo placeholder on the About Me page and it will automatically resize to fit the small image.

User Tip: Occasionally a photo will not automatically resize. You can either try a different photo, which will probably work or go to iPhoto® and resize a copy of the image for this purpose.

Album page after you add your choices

Now you already know how to add individual photos. Simply select the appropriate page and drag and drop the items on the placeholders; change your text and you are up and running. You can create your own movies with iMovies or download movies to your iTunes library and use them onyour website. This is explained in Chapter 4.

User Tip: Be certain you have the right to copy and publish photos and videos to your public website. It is always wisest to use your own original photos and videos to avoid copyright infringement,

Publishing your new website

To test your new website as you work on it in iWeb® without "going public" you can "publish" to a local folder it to see what it will look like on the web. This will show you how it looks and performs as a live site.

First, save your work. Under "File," scroll down to "save" and save the website. If you have added a lot of photos or albums, this could take a while. Be patient and let iWeb® do the job.

At the top left corner of the iWeb® window, you will see a red folder named "Site." Double-click on the word "site" and wait for it to be highlighted. Now type in a name for your new website and hit enter; as you do, you will notice that it appears over to the right in the larger window by "site name." Beside the "Publish to:" label is a drop-down menu that gives you three choices. For now, choose "local folder." You may want to create a new folder on your desktop called "My website." Under "Folder Location: choose the folder you created and be sure you open it. The path will show in the window and should include the folder name you used. For testing purposes, that is all you need to do. Now click on the green arrow icon at lower left that is labeled "Publish site." A drop down window will appear; click "continue". After a minute, you will see the message in Figure 11. Click "Visit Site Now"

Published site message

When you click on "visit site," your browser will launch and you will be able to move around your website just as the rest of the world will see it.

Now that you have the first version of your site done, it is time to customize and expand it. Even after your site is up on the web, making changes is fast and easy. Your website will grow and expand over time as you build your video and photo library or add to your blog. The fun is just beginning!

3 WORKING WITH THE INSPECTOR MENU

Now that you have created your personal website, you can make it more personalized and distinctively your own. The possibilities are endless. To get started, let us look at some of the features of the Inspector.

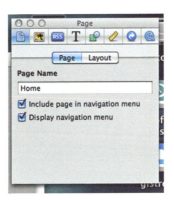

Page Inspector

The Inspector contains eight tabs across the top that give you many opportunities to customize your website.

On the "page" tab you have two sub-options: Page changes affect the whole page. You can also change the name of the page that will appear in the title and menu bar.

Experiment with changing the name and checking and unchecking the boxes until you feel comfortable making the changes. As long as you do not save the changes, you can always undo them.

Now, click on the "Layout" tab. You will now see the following image and discover a multitude of possibilities. We will go through each one.

Layout Inspector

Layout Options

Do not save any of the changes until you feel comfortable with these features.

You can change the spacing at the top and bottom of the page. Just for fun put "50 px" in the first box and see how it affects your page. Now change it back to "0 px"

Similarly, you can change any of the other settings and see how they affect your page. Generally, however, these are good settings.

Now look at "Page Background." The drop down menu offers "Color Fill" and three other choices. When you click on the white box, you will get a color palette and can change the color of your website.

The same options apply to the Browser Background selection. This is what shows around your webpage and fills the rest of the screen when someone looks at your site.

Play around with these options until you feel comfortable.

Look at the following image for ideas of how this works.

Modified page layout

This illustrates some of the options available to you. Scanning an image of rice paper backed by yellow construction paper made the yellow background. You can make any image you choose and use it for your website. See the chapter on
Customizing tricks for more details.

Adding Photos and Photo Pages

Besides the Album page you have added, you can also add a dedicated photo page. This is a great way to highlight special occasions or memorable events.

As an example, you might choose the Formal theme photo page and post your favorite wedding photograph with a short description. You can do the same for a vacation or birth of a child or grandchild.

In the left side menu highlight the word Photos and change it to the name you wish to use for your page: "Our Wedding" or "our new baby" for example. This name will appear in the menu bar of the web site.

Open the Media Menu and highlight Photos at the top.

Choose the individual photos you want to display on this page and drag and drop them on the placeholder photos on the page.

Drop each photo next to one already on the page. You can move them around on the page to arrange them as you wish.

To delete a photo simply click on it to highlight it and hit the delete key. It will still be in iPhoto® so do not worry about losing it.

By default, the title that appears in iPhoto® will be centered below each photo. Simply highlight it to change it to the description you want on your website. Click on the "Fonts" icon at the bottom of the iWeb® window to open the font menu and you can change the font, size and color of the captions.

After you have added several photos, you can click on one and a box will appear called "Photo Grid." This presents you with several options; you can choose the type of frame you want around your photos under "Album Style" as well as how many columns of pictures you want and the spacing, caption and number of photos per page.

Now go to your photo page, then open the Inspector panel at the top of the Inspector tool panel, and click on the image of the palm tree. This will open the Photo Inspector tools. If you do not want to allow your photos to be downloaded by others, click on "none", in the drop down menu.

Photo Inspector

Under "Photos," You can choose the download options you will allow your visitors. Check the drop down menu and decide if you will allow any downloads of your photos.

If you allow visitors to subscribe, they will be notified when you add photos to your page.

You can also allow people to post comments about your photos.

When you feel familiar with your options under the Photo tab, click on the "Slide Show" tab to see your options there

Slideshow Inspector

Creating your own Blog

Creating your own Blog is fun and a great way to share the events in your life with friends and family, especially if they are far away. It is easy to do with iWeb®. For purposes of this demonstration and for variety, choose a different theme for this page. Since this will be a newsletter type of blog, we will use the "Gazette" theme Blog template. Click on the Gazette theme and the Blog template. Some of the features on this Blog, will not appear on other theme blogs but you can add them if you wish. See the chapter on Customizing Tips for more information. For now, use this one to practice with and you can change it later.

pages in the menu to the left This gives you
the main blog page and a page where you do your entries as well as an
archive page which catalogs all of your past entries. Go to the original
blog page and give it a new name. You already know how to change the
photos and create links to your albums. You can change any of the entries
and captions to personalize the blog and make it yours. You may want to
change the heading "Listening to:" in the right side column to something
else such as "Places I have visited" and then list your travels below. One
suggestion that would make your blog interesting is to create links to your
friends and family who also have websites. It is easy and they would
probably appreciate it. You should ask their permission before you create
the link. The process is similar to linking to your photo albums.

Highlight the placeholder name "Sam" and type in the name of your friend
or family you wish to link to any little blurb below it. Now drag your
cursor over his or her name to highlight it.

Go to the Hyperlink Inspector tool and check the box that says "Enable as
a hyperlink"; choose "An external page" and then copy and paste the URL
for your friend's website in the window blow.

Check the box beside "open link in new window" and you are done. If you
do not have a small photo, you can replace the placeholder photo with any
image or just delete it altogether.

User Tip: To make a quick, easy link to another website, first open the
Hyperlink Inspector, then open that website in Safari and highlight the
URL at the top of your browser window, now highlight the words you
want to use for a link on your new web page.

You will notice that the URL of the website you are linking to appears automatically in the URL box of the Inspector when you check the "Enable as hyperlink" box and your link is all set. If you want to test the link, click off the worlds you highlighted, check the box in the Inspector that is beside "Make Hyperlinks Active" and then click on your new link. It will take you to that website. After you test the link, uncheck the "Make Hyperlinks Active" box until you are ready to publish.

You can change the photo to one of the persons you linked to or any other image you think is appropriate for them by dragging from iPhoto® and dropping just like you did with the photo page.

On the left side column, you can add your personal photo and fill in the information you want about yourself. You can change the categories or eliminate them altogether if you wish. For security reasons, I chose to leave out my birthday since that is often used as an identifier. Near the bottom of the left column, is a link "View Complete Profile/" Simply highlight the phrase, retype it to make it active and then go to the Hyperlink Inspector and link it to your "About Me" page.

As you continue to build your web site, you can add more links to other areas and pages. Do not worry if you do not replace all the placeholder photos and words right now; you can continue to change and edit this and all the other pages as you work on your site. There are several other settings you will want to deal with before you finish your blog setup. Go to the Blog Inspector tool and look at the options.

Blog Inspector

The Blog main page will show excerpts from your blog entries. You can set the number of excerpts that will be displayed.

You can also set the length of each excerpt-usually just a paragraph or two.

Do you want to allow your readers to comment on your blog entries? If so, check the box and decide if you will allow them to include attachments such as photos or other graphics. **Note:** The comments will appear without you having to approve them first.

If you allow a search field to be displayed, readers can search through your blog archive for specific subjects or words.

The next tab is the Podcast tool. If you would like to add pod casts to your website, check the help menu and GarageBand in your Applications folder for more information

Writing a Blog Entry

In the left side menu of iWeb®, under the Blog icon is an icon labeled "Entries." When you click on it, a new page appears that has placeholder text and a photo. If you have not already done so, change the Header to you own on both the Blog page and the Entries page. Change the photo to one of yours by dragging and dropping. Now highlight the entry title and give it a new one.

Next, highlight the text and start typing your thoughts

for your first blog entry. You will notice that the date appears automatically. Here is your blank canvas to express your thoughts and feelings on any topic you choose. You determine what to discuss and how you want the world to see you through your writing.

Watch the magic: Now that you have finished your entry, go back to the Blog page and you will notice that your entry is there for people to read. If you go to "Archive," you will see your entry listed by title and date. Each entry you create will behave the same way and your blog will grow as you write.

When you are ready to add a new entry, simply go to the "Entries" page and click on "Add Entry", Copy and Paste your header from your previous page, change the photo and caption and start writing your new blog entry.

Changing Page Names, Headers and Text

Look at the Text Inspector tool, which is the next tab at the top of the inspector menu, the letter "T." For this exercise, go to your "Home" or "Welcome" page.

Double click on the heading "Welcome to My Site" at the top of the web page. Using the text Inspector, you can dress this up and give it more impact. For now, change the text color to gold and the background to burgundy. Open the Font tool located at lower right and choose a font and style. By highlighting your header and sliding the insert margin bar, you can add more spacing around your header. If you followed these steps, your website should look like this with the words still highlighted.

Text options applied to a page header

All of these options can be applied to any text on your website. You can choose any font, style and color you like and make as many different looks as you wish.

Click on the next tab at the top and you will open the Graphic Inspector. Experiment with highlighting different text boxes and making changes. You can add borders, background colors, make sections appear in relief and many other special effects to personalize your site even more. Here are some examples:

Graphic Inspector

The next tab is an image of a ruler and is the Metrics Inspector. This tool allows you to manipulate your graphics and text in many different ways. Choose one of your images and try flipping and rotating it as well as resizing and moving it around the page. Here is an example of the power of this tool: Take some time to explore the possibilities. See more ideas in the chapter on Customizing Tips and Tricks.

Metric Inspector

The final tab in the inspector menu is the QuickTime Inspector. This is the place where you can control both movie and audio files. For demonstration purposes, open your Audio files in the Media menu and choose any song or audio file you like. Drag and drop it to your welcome page just below the text. A large box will appear with a control bar at the bottom and a gray area containing the message "Drag Image Here." You can make this box small by dragging the corner of the box inward toward its center. You can click on your photo tab and choose any image you like to fill the box. Now close the Media tab and click on the image you have added to the welcome page. Open the Inspector again and be sure you are on the QuickTime Inspector menu: the last tab on the upper right. You should have a desktop that looks similar to the following:

QuickTime Inspector

You will notice that the first slide bar controls where the "movie," or in this case, the song begins and ends. You do not have to play the entire piece; if you wish to play just a short snippet, you can do that. The next slide bar chooses which frame of a video you want to display in the image birthday party for example, you could choose the moment the honored guest blows out the candles as the "poster" that is displayed on the page.

Because we are using an audio file, that option is not available here. There are three other settings available in this inspector. Click on the box on your web page that represents the movie or audio file you are working with so that the sizing tabs surround it, and then you can choose to have the song play automatically (Autoplay), loop back and continue to play and you can choose to show or not show the control bar at the bottom of the image. If you click the play icon on the control bar on your web page, you will be able to hear how it will sound to your visitors. All of these settings are also available to your video files.

When you add audio and video files, be sure they are files that you own the rights to. Do not post other people's intellectual property to your website without permission. When you post your website to the web, you are "publishing" and must own the rights to all the material on your site.

4 THE MENU BAR

The menu bar across the top of the iWeb® screen will lead you to most of the features of iWeb®. From here, you can view and modify nearly every feature of your website. For the demonstration, leave your iWeb® open to the Welcome or Home page. Take a moment and explore each drop down menu across the top of the screen. Most of the items will seem familiar and be readily understood as to their function. A few, however, would benefit from some explanation. Starting on the left of the menu bar, look at the "File" drop down menu.

File menu options

File Menu Options

Scanning down the list on this menu reveals a few new options. Several of these options are also available in the icon menu at the bottom of the iWeb® page. Most of the choices are intuitive.

You can publish your site and update it by just publishing the changes you have made. You can visit your site and see it the way the public will. If you are keeping a blog that allows comments, you can check for new comments by clicking on that option. Now, we are down to the truly unique options under the file menu.

Set Up Google AdSense is a powerful option that allows you to support your website with advertising from Google. It is quite easy and fast to set up and, depending on how much traffic your website generates, could provide some help in supporting your new site. If you already have a Google AdSense account, you will see a window like this:

Google existing account window

Simply enter your information and click "submit". If you do not already have an account, you will see this window when you click Create a new account:

Google AdSense new account

Again, just fill in your email and click on Submit. In both cases, you will be walked through setting up your AdSense account and Google will teach you how to place the ads using the Google widget in iWeb®. You will find the widget in the media tool panel.

Setting up a MobileMe account and Domain Name

The next option in the File menu is to host your personal domain name at MobileMe. Of course, first you must have a MobileMe account. Setting that up is easy.

Go to System Preferences and click on the MobileMe icon. Apple® will walk you through the set-up process. Once you have finished that, you can use MobileMe to host your website. It is cheap, easy and secure. Simply follow the instructions at http://docs.info.apple.com/article.html?path=MobileMe/Account/en/acct17 114.html

To set up your domain name on MobileMe, go to your MobileMe account and follow the instructions. If you need more assistance, follow the instructions at the Apple® website at:

http://www.apple.com/mobileme/setup/pc.html

Edit Menu options

The Edit menu is familiar and you will recognize the available options there so move over to the Insert menu.

Insert Menu

This menu presents several new choices. Placing your cursor where you would like a new text box and choosing Insert>Text will result in a new typing location that you can move around the page and increase or decrease the size as needed. See the example above.

Insert>Shape is a powerful tool that allows you to significantly change the appearance of your web page. On your home page below the text box, choose a place to put your cursor on a blank space on the page. Choose a shape and play with sizing it and changing it by moving the little squares on the sides. Once you have a size and shape you want, you can drag and drop a photo into it and it will fit the space.

Insert>Shape

When you choose the oval, a small circle will appear on you page in the area where your cursor is. You can drag this shape to any spot on your webpage. You can also click on the little squares on each side and change the shape and size of the shape. If you wish, you can fill it with a color or pattern. In the following example, I chose a gold color and an Advanced Gradient fill.

Shape Insert

The next item in the Insert list is Button. This option gives pre-defined buttons to use on your page. By default, the "Made on a MAC" button appears on the bottom of each page; if you do not want that to appear, you can delete it. When you are working on a pod cast or Blog page, the subscription buttons are available. On all pages, the email and counter buttons are available. When you insert the button, you may move it to your preferred place on the page. When the website is active, the buttons will be live and the viewer can click on the email link to contact you. The next item, "Widget," will be explained in the next chapter.

Format options

Move to the right to the Format tab. Again, there are several options that are unique to iWeb®. Highlight a block of text and then click on Format>Font and you will be given several options that determine the type characteristics and spacing. You can apply these settings to the entire page or to selected text.

One of the most powerful features of this menu option is the Mask function. Select a photo on one of your web pages (do not choose one on your album or photo page) and then select Format>Mask and you will immediately see a box appear on the photo. This will allow you to change the size and position of the area of the photo you use for your page. Undo the selections you have made and select the photo again and go to Format>Mask with Shape and choose a shape for your image. You can size the mask as you need and move the image within the mask to achieve the desired look. Here is a webpage with an oval mask over the ship photo. Notice that the reflection matches the image.

Mask with Shape

User Tip: The mask function will not work on your album or photo pages. It is designed to work with photos and illustrations you use to build your web pages such as the welcome page above.

Using the bottom menu The menu across the bottom of the iWeb® window, contains several icon buttons that can help you navigate around the program. Most of the icons are self-explanatory; for example, "Add Page" and "Publish Site" do exactly that. The "Visit" icon will take you to your published site on the web.

Some functions, such as "Text Box" and "Shapes" will insert a box or shape you can move around and resize to suit your needs. "Mask" and "Rotate" become active and available when you have an image or photo highlighted on the page you are working on. If you have a mask, such as an oval over a photo, the icon title will change automatically to "Unmask." The "Adjust" icon will give you a very powerful tool for editing your photos within iWeb®. The remaining tools to the right of the bottom bar will be familiar and are the ones you will probably use most often.

There is one icon left in the default bottom menu bar. The "Theme" icon has a special function because it can allow you to test themes as you work on your web page. If you click once on the icon, it will open a window that shows all the themes available. One theme will be faint and not available to you. You are currently using that theme. You can "test" any of the other themes on the existing web page. Some items will not be positioned correctly and you can move them around if you wish. If you do not like the page, go to Edit>Undo Change Theme to return to the original page.

5 WIDGETS

The Widget tool is incredibly easy and powerful. There are widgets for a variety of functions that expand and enhance your website for both you and your readers. In this chapter, we will try to work with some of these magic tools

Widget Tools

The Widget menu shows nine different tools available to enhance your website.

Be patient and take the time to experiment with them until you feel comfortable and understand how each one works.

Start with the Google Maps widget. For practice, choose a blank web page; I am using the Black theme blank page. I put a title at the top, "Playing with Widgets." Since this is just for practice and we do not intend to publish this page, you can do anything you want here. Click on the Google Maps widget and you will be presented with the default map and a toolbar to customize it.

Map widget

You can enter the address you want to show on your website in the box. For example, if you enter "10 Downing St. London, England" in the Address box, it will automatically correct the format and show the location on the map when you click the "Apply" button. You may also check and uncheck the options shown below the address box. Click on the edge of the map to get the sizing arrows and size the map to suit your needs. Drag the map to any position on the page and add a text box above or below it to write your personal comments.

The MobileMe Gallery widget is similar. If you have a MobileMe account with albums you have posted there, it will automatically connect and give you a drop-down menu of the galleries available. Simply choose the one you want to feature on your page and size the window to fit your page. Again, you can add a text box to write your narration of the slide show that will automatically run on your website when visitors click on the gallery image.

User Tip: Modern cameras record a lot of information that will be available to viewers of images you post to the web, either on your site or somewhere else. This can include location of the photo. Be certain you consider this when you post photos anywhere on the web.

If you have a favorite YouTube video or one that you have posted on YouTube, you can include it in your website by pasting or typing the URL in the space provided when you drag the YouTube widget to your webpage. It will appear in its own window and allow you to size it to fit your layout. You can also add text and other related links. That is what the YouTube widget does.

The Countdown widget offers a great way to build anticipation for an upcoming event. The options window gives you a chance to personalize it for your webpage. Like all widgets, you can drag, drop and resize to fit your own design.

With the RSS and HTML widgets, you can add subscribing links and other live content from other websites to your page. In both cases, you can either copy and paste or simply type in the appropriate code. As you experiment with the widgets, you will find they offer a lot of power and options to your web design.

HTML Widget

One widget that will become very important to managing your web site is the HTML Snippet. This tool will allow you to add snippets of HTML (Hypertext Markup Language) code to your web page. You do not have to understand programming code or be a programmer of HTML to use it in your website. There are many instances where you will be given snippets of code to place in your web site. If you choose to run Amazon ads on your web pages, you will use HTML Snippets. Often, a video will give you the opportunity to embed code on your web page. The owner of the video is encouraging you to "spread the word" about a product or service.

If you visit the website http://web.me.com/GLStrout/GLStrout/Welcome.html you will see HTML links used in the ads, the link to the Personal Homepage Ring, the Hubpages and some of the videos. For instance, the video of the Tesla Model S is an HTML snippet.

When you are offered a snippet for your website, simply copy and paste it into the black snippet edit box that appears when you drag the widget to your web page. After you paste the snippet into the edit box, click "apply" and the snippet will be activated. You may not see the ad or other item until you publish the change to your web site. After publishing again, visit your site and confirm that the snippet is working as you expected.

6 PUBLISHING OPTIONS

If you followed the steps in Chapter 1, you have already "published" your site to a local folder, which means no one but you can see it. Now that you have finished your site and want to share it with the world, it is time to consider how to get your site launched. First, be sure to review your site and spell-check it so that you make the best possible impression. Save all the changes and give it one last test by re-publishing it to a local folder. Refer to Chapter 1 for information that is more detailed.

Option 1: MobileMe

Perhaps the easiest and probably the cheapest way to host your website is to use MobileMe. The "cloud" or Internet based service provider by Apple®, Inc. is quick, convenient and secure. You will need to sign up for MobileMe, which will offer you a free 60-day trial membership. For less than $10 per month, membership includes 20 gigabytes of storage for your website, mail, calendar, address book, iDisk backup storage and photo gallery. The annual cost is $99.00 US. There is additional storage available you can add if you need it. I recommend not buying the extra storage at the time of sign-up because you may never use it. To set up your account, go to www.me.com.

Choosing your member name becomes important here. Whatever you choose, will be part of your web address. You may want to use some form of your own name. Consider a web address that reflects your goal in creating a website. Also, if you intend to publish more than one site on your account, that member name will appear in the URL (web address) of each website. You may also provide your own URL such as www.[yourname].com.

Once you have your MobileMe account set up, go to the iWeb® page titled "Site Publishing Settings" and fill in the information that it asks for. You will find this page at the top of the left menu bar; it is the cloud symbol. If you wish, you can link your website with your Facebook page by checking the box. When you finish entering the information, click the green arrow at the bottom of the iWeb® screen and it will publish your site for the world to see. This process will take a few minutes depending on how big your site is, so be patient. When the publication is done, it will give you the option to visit your new site.

Option 2: FTP Server

To use this option, you will need to set up an account with a web hosting service such as Dream Host, http://www.dreamhost.com, or any other hosting service. They will usually also offer you an opportunity to register your own domain name. A domain name is the web address you use for your website and email such as www.johndoe.com. There will be some fee involved but it will allow you to have your own personal exclusive domain and web address.

Again, once you have set up the account and have your FTP account established, go to the iWeb® page and fill in the blanks on the "Site Publishing Settings" screen. After you fill in the information, you can click the "test connection" button to verify that it works properly. Your hosting service should tell you which options you will need to make the connection work properly. Click on the green "publish site" arrow and the program will do the rest. This may take some time to get up and running, but just follow the instructions on the screen and it will not be difficult. If you do have trouble, contact your hosting service for assistance.

Option 3: Local Folder

This allows you to keep a copy of your published site on your home computer. It is the option you used in Chapter 1 to test your site and see how it would look and operate when you publish it. I recommend you continue to publish your site to your local folder as a means of back up and testing. Create a new folder just for your website and periodically publish to it as your site grows and changes.

Adding a Facebook® Link

Adding a Facebook® link is easy with iWeb®. Go to the Site Publishing Settings page by clicking on the site name. Scroll down to the Facebook® and check the box beside the phrase "Update my Facebook® profile when I publish this site." The program will ask you for your login information and ask you to approve access to your account information. Simply approve that and you can either check the box that tells it to keep you logging in or you can choose to log in each time you update. You can stop the updates by clicking on the "Remove Account" button at any time.

Each time you update your website all of your contacts on Facebook will be able to see the new features on your website. Facebook will help to drive traffic to your website.

Bringing People to Your Web Site

Now that you have built this wonderful web site, how do you get people to notice it? The number one answer is Facebook®. Use the link in iWeb to connect your website to your Facebook account. Every time you write a blog entry or make any other update to your website, a notice will appear for all of your friends and contacts on Facebook® so that they can visit your site and see what you are doing. This is an excellent way to announce the new artwork or article you have created or the new product you are selling.

Another method of generating traffic is to sign up for Google Adwords. For very little money, you can run a Google ad. If you are selling a product or service, this will bring interested people to your site. Also, consider using a program such as iWeb SEO (Search Engine Optimization) Tool to help you add tags to your web site that will help search engines such as Bing and Google to find your site. See the link in the Appendix.

Consider signing up for a web ring. This is a group of connected websites that lead visitors from one similar site to another. The ring may be a group of art, sports, writing or business web sites that share a common interest. For a personal or family website consider a ring such as Personal Homepage Ring.

Supporting your web site

While it is true that posting a web site on MobileMe is very inexpensive, it is always helpful if you can either do it for nothing or perhaps even make a few dollars in the process. You have that option available with iWeb®.

The easiest way to generate income from your web site is to use Google AdSense®. In the chapter on the top menu bar, we discussed setting up AdSense®. Once you have the account established with Google, go to the Widgets menu and drag the AdSense widget to a web page. You can choose the size and shape of the ad and place it where you want the ad to appear on your site. You can also choose a background color that will look good on your page. When you are satisfied with the ad layout, save the web site in iWeb® and choose publish site changes from the file menu. When your site goes live, an ad from Google will appear on your web page. Each time people click on the ad, it will generate a small income to your AdSense® account.

Consider another possible source of income for your site. If you become an Amazon Associate, you can use the HTML widget to set up Amazon.com ads. This will also generate income when people click on the ads and then buy from Amazon. In both cases, the ad content will be determined by the content on your web page and will change each time someone visits the site. You cannot generate income by clicking on the ads yourself; Google and Amazon will know, and you may lose your accounts. You can, however, encourage others to make use of the ad to help support the site.

7 CUSTOMIZING YOUR SITE

Making changes to your published site is easy and fast. Simply go to iWeb® and change the saved webpage or add a new entry to your blog. Then choose File>Publish Site Changes and the site will be updated. Be sure your "Publish to" setting is correct.

I like to save my site each time I make a change and periodically publish it to a local folder as a second backup.

When you publish your site to the web, it will take significantly longer to process than it did to publish to a local folder. Be patient.

If you edit a photo outside of iWeb® or iPhoto®, it may not show in the media photo menu in iWeb® until you quit iPhoto® and re-launch it.

Occasionally the Hyperlink will not automatically fill in the URL in the Inspector when you are trying to make a new link. Simply copy the URL from the browser and paste it into the link window on the inspector.

When you have added a number of photos to your pages, it will take some time to save. After the first time, choose "save changes" from the file menu and it will be faster.

After you visit your site to test it and then make changes in iWeb®, Quit your browser and re-launch it to be sure the change are reflected when you visit your site again.

Adding albums for special events like weddings and anniversaries or holiday gatherings is an effective way to highlight the event. Adding a photo page with your favorite photos that can be displayed in a slideshow can add special interest to your site.

If you have large albums in iPhoto®, you may want to create new, smaller edited albums to use on your web site. It is easier to edit and arrange in iPhoto® than in iWeb®.

You can dress up the menu bar and make it more useable by inserting a text box above it and adding the word "Menu". See an example at http://web.me.com/GLStrout/GLStrout/Welcome.html To make room for the new text box, simply go to View>Show Layout and then grab the box containing the menu bar and drag it down enough to give room for the new text box.

Creating your own patterns and backgrounds

It is easy to create unique and interesting backgrounds and patterns in iWeb®. In figure 14, you will notice that the background that will appear behind the web page is bright yellow and seems to have a pattern on it. The pattern was created using a sheet of rice paper over a piece of yellow construction paper. We then scanned in the image and made a small image to use for the web page.

This is an example of rice paper over blue construction paper. There is no limit to the patterns you can create.

To change a background on your web site, open the Inspector tool and choose the first tab for the page inspector; choose Layout. From this inspector, you can control the overall appearance of your web page. For now, skip the first section that deals with page size. After you have launched your site, you can experiment with these settings if you wish but, generally, it is just as well to leave the default settings. Go to the Page Background section. You will see that you have several different options for the page you are working on. By mixing and matching the combinations for the two drop-down menus, you can change the effect of the image you choose. The same is true for the Browser Background; however, the options are more limited because of the variation in screen size and browser characteristics. Experiment with these options. They will allow you to have a truly unique web page. Remember that the more complex the image, the longer it will take for the page to load.

Experiment and practice with your web design. You will discover many new and exciting ways to improve your website. Be patient and have fun. It may take a little time to learn all the tricks but the rewards will be worth it.

Useful Links

Apple, Inc. has a tremendous amount of useful information.

IWeb SEO Tool

Personal Homepage Ring

Commercial template sites

There are several places on the Internet that will sell you a theme template. Here are just a few examples:

IWeb® template.com

iWeb® Themes Park

One of the best sites for iWeb® users is All About iWeb®. It will inspire you to try many more complicated tricks ad customizations.

ABOUT THE AUTHOR

Freelance author George L. Strout started programming on Apple IIe computers when they were the latest and greatest technology. Over the years, he has worked in several different computer languages and on each generation of Apple computer as it came on the market.

He believes that Apple, Inc.'s iWeb program is one of the most under-appreciated features of the current product line.

Follow his current writing projects and blog at his personal website.

Also, visit the author's page at Smashwords

www.ingramcontent.com/pod-product-compliance
Lightning Source LLC
Chambersburg PA
CBHW041146050326
40689CB00001B/504